"At last, Louie Giglio has put into print the message God birthed in him years ago…a message that has shaped a generation of students, a message that has sent shock waves through the church, a message that has the potential to profoundly impact your worship."

ANDY STANLEY, PASTOR, NORTH POINT COMMUNITY CHURCH AND AUTHOR OF *THE NEXT GENERATION LEADER*

"I'm not a worship guy…*er,* or so I thought, but Louie's book nailed me. After reading this, I finally "get" worship. Louie helped me realize that worship is an all-the-time thing, a *life* thing. I am encouraged by his book. Mostly, I am moved by Louie's obvious passion for God and his gift for making worship make sense."

MICHAEL YACONELLI, OWNER, YOUTH SPECIALTIES

"Some of the most inspiring teaching on worship I've ever heard has come from the mouth of Louie Giglio. Having read *The Air I Breathe,* I can now say the same of Louie's gift to communicate through the *written* word. This book has inspired me as a worshiper and as a worship leader."

MATT REDMAN, AUTHOR OF *THE UNQUENCHABLE WORSHIPPER* AND *THE HEART OF WORSHIP*

"Don't read *The Air I Breathe* unless you want to reexamine your life to see whom or what you are truly worshiping on a daily basis."

BILLY RAY HEARN, FOUNDER, SPARROW RECORDS

"Louie Giglio explores what God desires most in our worship with clarity and insight. Upon reading *The Air I Breathe,* you'll be both challenged and liberated to discover that true worship inescapably involves who you are—all the time."

DR. CHARLES F. STANLEY, SENIOR PASTOR,
FIRST BAPTIST CHURCH, ATLANTA, GEORGIA

"Louie Giglio communicates Christian truth in a wonderfully accessible and relevant way. *The Air I Breathe* is packed full of gems that inspire and encourage."

MIKE PILIVACHI, PASTOR, SOUL SURVIVOR CHURCH,
WATFORD, UNITED KINGDOM

"This book is a challenging reminder that our worship is for God and not for ourselves."

BILL HEARN, PRESIDENT AND CEO,
EMI CHRISTIAN MUSIC GROUP

THE AIR I BREATHE

[worship as a way of life]

LIFECHANGE BOOKS

LOUIE GIGLIO

Multnomah® Publishers *Sisters*, Oregon

THE AIR I BREATHE
published by Multnomah Publishers, Inc.

© 2003 by Louie Giglio
International Standard Book Number: 1-59052-153-6

Cover image by Wataru Yanagida/Photonica

Unless otherwise indicated, Scripture quotations are from:
The New American Standard Bible® © 1960, 1977, 1995
by the Lockman Foundation. Used by permission.
Other Scripture quotations are from:
The Holy Bible, New International Version (NIV)
© 1973, 1984 by International Bible Society,
used by permission of Zondervan Publishing House;
The Message © 1993 by Eugene H. Peterson;
and *The Holy Bible,* King James Version (KJV).

Multnomah is a trademark of Multnomah Publishers, Inc.,
and is registered in the U.S. Patent and Trademark Office.
The colophon is a trademark of Multnomah Publishers, Inc.

Printed in the United States of America

For information:
MULTNOMAH PUBLISHERS, INC. • P.O. BOX 1720 • SISTERS, OR 97759

Library of Congress Cataloging-in-Publication Data

Giglio, Louie.
  The air I breathe / by Louie Giglio.
      p. cm.
    ISBN 1-59052-153-6
    1. Worship.   I. Title.
    BV10.3.G54 2003
    248.3—dc21

                                                      2003000491

03 04 05 06 07 08—10 9 8 7 6 5 4 3 2 1 0

Anyone who knows me knows
Shelley is a vital part of who I am
and all I do...including this little book.
Together we want our lives to count for His renown.
Shelley, you are an amazing,
God-sent partner in life, love, laughter,
and ministry — in worship.

Table of Contents

Chapter 1

THAT THING WE DO

You, my friend…are a worshiper!

There, I said it.

Everyday, all day long, in every place, you worship. It's what you do. It's who you are.

So if by chance you have only a few seconds to glance at this book, that's what it's all about. We are all worshipers, created to bring pleasure and honor to the God who made us.

You may not consider yourself a "worshiping" kind of person, but you cannot help but worship…something.

It's what you were made to do.

Should you for some reason choose not to give God what He desires, you'll worship anyway—simply exchanging the Creator for something He has created.

Whatever's Worth Most

Think of it this way: Worship is simply about value. The simplest definition I can give is this: Worship is our response to what we value most.

That's why worship is that thing we all do. It's what we're all about on any given day. Worship is about saying, "This person, this thing, this experience (this whatever) is what matters most to me...it's the thing of highest value in my life."

That "thing" might be a relationship. A dream. A position. Status. Something you own. A name. A job. Some kind of pleasure. Whatever name you put on it, this "thing" is what you've concluded in your heart is worth most to you. And whatever is worth most to you is—you guessed it—what you worship.

Worship, in essence, is declaring what we value most. As a result, worship fuels our actions, becoming the driving force of all we do.

And we're not just talking about the religious crowd. The Christian. The churchgoer among us. We're talking about everybody on planet earth. A multitude of souls proclaiming with every breath what is worthy of their affection, their attention, their allegiance. Proclaiming with every step what it is they worship.

Some of us attend the church on the corner, professing to worship the living God above all. Others, who rarely darken the church doors, would say worship isn't a part of their lives because they aren't "religious." But everybody has an altar. And every altar has a throne.

So how do you know where and what you worship?

It's easy. You simply follow the trail of your time, your affection, your energy, your money, and your allegiance. At the end of that trail you'll find a throne; and whatever, or whomever, is on that throne is what's of highest value to you. On that throne is what you worship.

Sure, not too many of us walk around saying, "I worship my stuff. I worship my job. I worship this pleasure. I worship her. I worship my body. I worship me!"

But the trail never lies. We may say we value this thing or that thing more than any other, but the volume of our actions speaks louder than our words.

In the end, our worship is more about what we do than what we say.

EVERYWHERE—WORSHIP

Worship is *the* activity of the human soul.

So not only do all people worship, but they worship all the time. Worship isn't just a Sunday thing. It's an all-the-time thing.

Right this very instant, all across

Worship is the activity of the human soul.

your city or town, people of all shapes and sizes, people of every age and purpose are doing it—continually <u>making decisions based on what they value most</u>. Worship happens everywhere…all day long.

In fact, some of the purest forms of worship are found outside the walls of the church and have no reference to the God of all creation. All you have to do is drop in on a concert at the local arena or take in a sporting event at a nearby stadium to see amazing worship. People are going for it: lifting their hands, shouting with joy, staking their claim, standing in awe, declaring their allegiance. Interestingly, these venues are filled with the same forms of worship mentioned in the pages of God's Word—the same expressions of worship that God desires.

Several years ago, watching an interview Oprah was doing with Michael Jackson, I was stunned with the reality of this truth. What I witnessed as she showed a video clip of people responding to him in concert settings around the world absolutely floored me. Talk about amazing worship!

In multiple cultures, throngs of people numbering into the hundreds of thousands were glued as one to his every move. On every continent they assembled like an army, waving their hands in the air. Some fell to their knees. Others strained with outstretched hands, hoping for a brief touch from his. Seared in my mind is the image of one young girl with a look on her face of total awe.

I couldn't believe it. What I was watching was some of the most intense worship I'd ever seen…anywhere. Far more "full-on" than much of what I'd experienced inside the church.

And for what? Granted, Michael Jackson is one of the best entertainers of our time, but he's not a great god. Yet the worship was phenomenal, demonstrating the God-given capacity for adoration that is rooted in the soul of every man.

CONNECTIVITY, PREWIRED

In the same way, we all worship something all the time. And you know what? We're really good at it.

If you think about it, history has known no shortage of worship. The timeline of mankind is littered with trillions of little idols. Every culture, every corner of earth, every age has had its gods. Just circle the globe and watch for worship. Study the great civilizations and explore their temples.

The compelling question for me is, "Why?" Why do we crave something to worship? Why are we so insatiably drawn from idol to idol, desperately needing something to champion, something to exalt, something to adore?

How do we know for sure that some things are more important than others, more worthy of worship? How do we even know that value, beauty, and worth exist?

I think it's because we were designed that way. We were made *for God*.

The Bible says it this way: All things were made *by* Him; and all things were made *for* Him.*

You've been created by God. And if that wasn't enough, you've also been created *for* Him. As a result, there's an internal homing device riveted deep with your soul that perpetually longs for your Maker. An internal, God-ward magnet, pulling your being toward Him.

Stamped in God's image, we know that there's something we attach to, something we fit with, someone we belong to, somewhere called home.

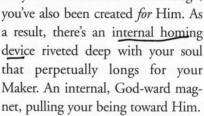

We come from the womb equipped for connectivity with God, prewired to praise.

That's why we come from the womb equipped for connectivity with God, prewired to praise. And that's why, from the youngest age, we begin to worship.

We arrive in this world as objects of divine affection, miraculous receptors designed to bring Him pleasure. If only everyone could *know* we've been created by and for God! If only we could all comprehend that we're precious to Him, housing mirrored souls designed to reflect His glory.

---

* You can find source information for this and other quotations in the back of this book.

THE QUESTION THAT CAPTIVATES US ALL

As I'm writing, my flight home to Atlanta is climbing high above the Chicago night. Staring out across the horizon, I'm captivated by the thousands of tiny lights, dotting the landscape as far as I can see. Countless twinkling stars of earth, hundreds of thousands of beacon lights. It's like a sea of little lights—streetlights, headlights, house lights, neon lights...all kinds of lights.

And I'm thinking, everywhere I see lights, there are people. People everywhere. A sea of humanity. And every single person down there is someone created with amazing potential and purpose. All uniquely fashioned to reflect back to their Creator His beauty and wonder. Each one breathing the air of earth in common accord. Each person given life...to give Him praise.

And that's only the view in one direction, looking out over just one city, in just one state, in one nation, on one continent.

I'm floored. As we jet through the darkened sky, I think of how this earth is home to billions of worshipers, created to light the darkness with stories of who He is. With echoes of all He has done.

But do they know it? Do *you* know it? Do you know in this moment that you were made by and for God?

While we soar over Chicago, our plane is just a little tiny speck to anyone who might look up and see us, a little dot of light blinking its way through the night. Yet onboard tonight are even more people. People everywhere.

Across the aisle from me, a middle-aged woman is digging into a well-worn Bible. (No, I'm not making this up!) She's leaning forward as she reads, as if she knows this book holds some secret key. I'm thinking how the same God who's worthy of all the earth's worship is the author of the very pages in her hands. She's holding the autobiographical revelation of His heart to mankind. There before her eyes is the extension of God's hand. And she's devouring it in large chunks, miraculously forgoing another showing of *My Big Fat Greek Wedding*. It's as if somehow within its pages she has discovered life's very meaning.

It seems we are all eventually captivated by the question of why. Why are we here? Is there a reason for our lives? Is there something we're uniquely destined to do?

It's the age-old dilemma—what's the purpose of life?

The answer begins and ends with God. Simply put, you and I were made by Him and made for Him. You exist for one purpose alone—to reflect back to God His matchless glory. And the experience of that one purpose is the truth we're all seeking.

Okay, to be fair, things have changed onboard. Forty minutes have passed and the woman across the aisle is now reading a David Baldacci novel, sending occasional glances toward the movie monitor.

Uh oh. The headphones are going on. I think she's being sucked into the movie.

Apparently, she's seen *My Big Fat Greek Wedding* a dozen times and is having little difficulty jumping right into the flow. It hasn't been thirty seconds and she's already laughing. (Not as loudly as the guy in front of me mind you, who with headphones on is loudly giving a blow-by-blow commentary of each scene to the stranger trapped beside him.)

I guess tonight won't see my miracle after all. The "little movie engine that could" wins again. The unstoppable force of *Big Fat Greek* rambles on. But she still gets major credit for her deep dive into the pages of God's Word. For she—just like the rest of us—is seeking God. And, as far as I can tell, finding Him on a plane to Georgia.

The guy next to me is sound asleep. The lady up front is talking in what sounds like a South African accent. The flight attendant buzzing around is tall and Romanian. A businessman behind me is wide awake and feverishly working.

All these people.

Do they know?

Do you?

Chapter 2

SOMETHING MORE

I think people know there's something more, though I have no clue if they know who He is.

A quick glance at history tells me we have always been searching.

In the New Testament book of Acts, a historical overview of the expansion of the early Christian church, we find the main character, Paul, entering Athens to proclaim the gospel. Right smack in the middle of the intellectual center of the known world, Paul found Athens to be a "city full of idols."

In fact, Paul found a multitude of idols to gods of every name and description. But one idol seized his heart, quickly becoming the focus of his message to the Athenian people. The inscription on this altar read, "TO AN UNKNOWN GOD."

Even with all their idols and altars, these intellectual and cultural giants wanted to cover their bases, making sure all deities were happy in the event there was something, or someone, more. The altar "UNKNOWN" stood among them, just in case it turned out that another object of worship was superior to all the others.

Intrigued by Paul's preaching, the council of moral overseers known as the Areopagus invited him to speak to their assembly. It didn't take Paul long to get to the point.

"Men of Athens," he began, crafting a simple and straight-to-the-heart response, "I see that you are religious in every respect. For passing through your objects of worship I also found an altar with this inscription, 'TO AN UNKNOWN GOD.' What you worship in ignorance, I proclaim to you."

Paul didn't find a worship-void in Athens. In fact, there was no apathy in their worship. Just uncertainty. Worshiping people wondering if there was something more.

A lot has changed since the Athens of old, its ancient idols and altars lie in ruins. But men everywhere are still searching...all the while building altars to everything under the sun. Wondering if there's a God you can know.

THE ULTIMATE SEARCH

God is always seeking you. Every sunset. Every clear blue sky. Each ocean wave. The starry host of night. He blankets each new day with the invitation, "I am here."

It's a kind of revelation accessible to all—God constantly exposing His creative power to anyone watching. Add to that the internal magnet we've already touched on, and you understand what it means when His Word says God has placed eternity in our hearts.

Somehow, we know He's there. The creation surrounding us tells us there's more to this life than living and dying.

Yet painted skies and a spinning earth aren't enough to tell His story. Heaven's hosts and atom's wonders…a revelation still incomplete. God's face couldn't be clearly known until His Son appeared—God on the ultimate search, appearing in human flesh. God coming down to restore and redeem fallen man.

God is always seeking you. He blankets each new day with the invitation, "I am here."

(To us, ready or not, Jesus came. To us, worthy or not, He appeared. Accepting or not, we find His footprints in Palestinian soil.

It's history. It's fact. It's inescapable. Jesus came. And in His own words, He came to "seek and to save that which was lost."

God wants you to know Him.

Searching for Him isn't like looking for a needle in a theological haystack. He isn't hiding. He isn't unknowable. He isn't some mysterious force or philosophical construct that you can't quite grasp or attain.

In fact, the opposite is true. His Son appeared to all in bodily form. Jesus, "the radiance of God's glory, the exact representation of his being," walking this earth in plain sight so that anyone seeking God could find their way to Him.

God's not hiding. He's been looking for you for a long, long time.

Do you know why? Because He wants you to know who He is...and who you are, too. He wants you to know that you're the object of His affection, created in His image, made by and for Him.

He wants you to know that the Unknown God has a name. He wants you to know that the incredible desire for worship rooted deep inside your heart was crafted for Him.

MEET GOD

Standing before the men of Athens, Paul took a deep breath and unfolded the mystery that his listeners had been searching for. He spoke of "the God who made the world and all things in it." Paul identified Him as "Lord of heaven and earth." And this God, Paul said, "gives to all people life and breath and all things."

Men of Athens, meet the God of gods.

Turns out they were right all along. There *was* another God greater than all their idols, higher than all the objects inhabiting all their altars.

This God is powerful enough, Paul proclaimed, to invent the whole world and everything it contains. And He "does not dwell in temples made by hands, nor is He served by human hands as though He needed anything." Turns out God doesn't live at the church after all. By the very logic of His immensity, He refuses to be contained by any temple or structure.

What a shame. I guess we have to say good-bye to the admonition we often give kids who get too rowdy at church—"SHHHhhhhhh! You're in *God's* house." Do we really believe that, or is it just a clever threat, a last resort after we've long since counted to three and still can't get the kids to settle down?

It does make for a nice image, though. Can you see Him at the door after the service, greeting everyone? "Thanks for coming, appreciate you coming, thanks for being here, glad you made it, hope you enjoyed it. Was everything okay? God bless. Oh yeah, *I'm* God—so, just...bless! Come back to see Me! Have a nice week!"

Is that God? Watching all the cars drive away, turning the church lights off, settling in for a long and quiet week, maybe playing a little on the organ, only to fling wide the doors again in seven days. "Hey! Glad you're back. Good to see you. Come on in!"

I don't think so. God doesn't have a church fetish. He probably cares less about the carpet color there than we think. Why? Because He's huge. Creator. Initiator of all things. Way too vast to be stuck in some building all week. Far too interested in our lives to simply watch us drive away from Him. Much more worthy of our time than just one hour of just one day.

This Unknown God is the all-sufficient God. He doesn't need a thing! He made the world and everything in it. Paul wanted the men of Athens to know that He's the constant supply of life, breath—everything!

And he wanted them to know that God is near.

NEAR...NOW

God is really close to you in this very moment. Right now, He's near.

Paul kept describing this huge and limitless God. He said God has "determined" for all human beings "their appointed times [the span of our lives] and the boundaries of their habitation [the details of our existence]..."

And all for what purpose? Check it out:

> ...that they [all people] would seek God, if per-
> haps they might grope for Him and find Him,

though He is not far from each one of us; for in
Him we live and move and exist.

No wonder the whole world is filled with worshipers.
Every last one of us has been created with a searching soul,
designed that way by God so that (as Augustine expressed
it) our hearts are restless until they
find their rest in Him.

If you've been wrestling with big
questions of ultimate truth, don't be
alarmed. If you feel at times like
you're inching your way through a
murky night in search of home,
you're not alone. The journey to God
can often feel like an awkward groping for someone our eyes cannot see.

That's why it's comforting to
know God is seeking you, too.

> Every last one
> of us has been
> created with a
> searching
> soul.

He's seeking you so you can know just how amazing
He is. He's seeking you so you can know what you're cre-
ated to do. He's seeking you so you can find Him and value
Him with all your heart.

He's seeking you because He's God...and He knows
you can't live without Him.

That, my friend, explains a ton of stuff for us.

For one, it explains why you worship and why you're so
good at it. It's why the whole world is worshiping even now.

And it explains why Jesus willingly came. He came to connect us to God and awaken us to the possibility of centering our worship on who and what matter most...forever.

Chapter 3

WHY WORSHIP MATTERS

When the subject is worship, the stakes are high—because worship is what God is all about.

Worship should matter to you simply because it matters to God. And worship matters to God because He knows He's worthy. I know that doesn't sound too persuasive in our me-centered culture, but it's true. Worship doesn't begin with us. Worship begins and ends with God. And God is worthy of all praise, from all people, for all time.

God is the center of everything that exists. Above all the little gods of earth, He alone is the Creator. Sustainer. Originator. Life Giver. Beauty Maker.

That's why every peek into His presence throughout the

pages of God's Word affirms that He dwells in endless praise.

Glimpse the angel host of Revelation, never ceasing to say, "Holy, holy, holy is the Lord God, the Almighty, who was and who is and who is to come." Never do they stop. Day and night they proclaim. Always affirming His infinite worth.

And "the heavens are telling of the glory of God; and their expanse is declaring the work of His hands." Why? Because that's what they were created to do, day after day— to tell God (and anyone else who's paying attention) that He is huge. All-powerful. Glorious. Limitless.

Beyond our wildest imagination.

And you know what's really wild? This massive God, who has never known any shortage of worship, wants to be worshiped…*by you.* Right now.

It's not that He needs any more worship to be worthy. No, God can't be more worthy than He already is and always has been. It's not that God needs our worship—but that He wants it. He wants it because He deserves it. And He commands it because to do so is the most loving thing He can possibly do.

God knows who He is. He knows what He's worth. And He knows that He has made us for His glory.

DON'T WASTE YOUR WORSHIP

Worship should matter to you because you are and always will be a worshiper. It's what you do. You can't help it. You can't stop it. You can't live without it. But you can choose where you invest it. You can choose to make your worship count for eternity.

We're created to worship. That's why you and I are going to spend our lives declaring the worth of something. As a result, we've got to make sure the thing we declare to be of greatest value is really worthy after all.

For me, I've got to keep making sure that what matters most—matters most to me.

The same is true of you. It's imperative that you find an object worthy of your affection. It's essential that you find a God worthy of your life's devotion.

You only have one life. And you only have one life of worship. You have one brief opportunity in time to declare your allegiance, to unleash your affection, to exalt something or someone above all else.

Don't waste your worship on some little god, squandering your birthright on idols made only with human imagination. Guard your worship…and carefully evaluate all potential takers.

To choose well doesn't mean we can't appreciate things of beauty and style. It's certainly not wrong to deeply love another. Nor is it a sin to value a great job or enjoy an amazing destination.

But when we elevate any of these things to the highest place in our hearts, we've gone too far.

For great is the LORD and most worthy of praise. He is to be feared above all gods. For all the gods of the nations are idols, but the LORD made the heavens. Splendor and majesty are before Him, strength and glory are in His sanctuary.

THE WAR FOR YOUR WORSHIP

Worship also matters because every day there's a battle for your worship.

The things we elevate. The values we serve. None of those choices are made in a vacuum. There's a war raging for our worship, and it's been raging since before there was time.

> Every day there's a battle for your worship.

Even before the earth was formed, one of God's highest angels bolted from His presence, refusing to join the ranks of the true worshipers, refusing to exalt God above all. The account records that in a flash Satan fell like lightning from heaven. Exalting himself more than God, Satan was banned from His presence.

Yet, having been in that presence, he knows God is central and worthy of all praise. He's heard the anthem. He's seen the glory.

But because of pride, he couldn't bow. Spurred on by self, he leads a band of fallen brothers, spreading his insurrection to as many as he can.

That's where we come in.

How does Satan advance his rebellion against God today? By contesting His supremacy throughout the earth, leading a traitor race to exchange "the truth of God for a lie," and to worship and serve "the creature rather than the Creator, who is blessed forever." Satan can't stop worship from happening, but he'll deceive anyone who lets him, leading them to empty wells and puny gods.

Let's check back in with Paul. Remember his message to the men of Athens? Remember his audience? The council Paul addressed that day was called the Areopagus, named after Ares, the Greek god of war. Isn't it interesting that this is the setting God chose for Paul to give this address on the real meaning of life? God's words of truth landed in the very arena where opinions battled.

In the same way, what God is saying to you will be challenged by the very fallen angels who challenged Him. That challenge is called temptation. Deception. Falsehood. Lies. Theft.

Do you know what God desires most from you? It's the one thing no other person on earth can give Him—your affection. Although a thousand other people can do the work, give the bucks, fill the gap…no one else can give God the unique affection that only you and He can share.

But just as much as God longs for your love, there's an enemy who seeks to steal it.

At this point, you may be saying, "I didn't start this war of worship—and I don't care to be in it. I just want to live my life, make my own choices, do my own thing."

That, however, is not an option. Our lives are on loan from God, a sacred trust of opportunities and decisions. And every one of our choices is made on a battlefield with heavenly ramifications.

The Last Temptation

Even Jesus faced the same fate.

Before going public with His ministry, He was led by God's Spirit into a wilderness challenge. Now, thirty years old, Jesus was preparing for all that was ahead by fasting for forty days and nights. He was learning what it means to depend on His Father. Clinging to Him for life itself.

As His fast was coming to a close, Jesus was physically drained but spiritually sharp. The enemy, no doubt seeing that Jesus looked weary, closed in with three potent temptations.

You remember the first: "If You're so hungry, turn these rocks into bread."

And the second: "If You're the Son of God, leap from the height of the temple. Surely Your Father will catch You long before You hit the ground."

But notice the last temptation. It was a takeover attempt for Christ's worship.

Satan offered Jesus all the world's kingdoms if Jesus would bow down and worship him. What on earth was Satan thinking? To ask the Son of God to bow down and worship a foolish exile of heaven, someone doomed to die, someone banished to an eternal future void of the beauty of angels' sounds—talk about being deceived!

> Whatever you worship, you imitate; whatever you imitate, you become.

Jesus' reply was clear. "It has already been written: Worship the Lord your God and serve Him only."

Your worship matters to God. If it didn't, Satan wouldn't care about stealing it from Him.

So keep your mind saturated with truth and diligently guard the temple of your heart.

BE CAREFUL WHAT YOU CHOOSE

There's one more reason worship should really matter to you—whatever you worship, you become.

You can worship whatever you want, but there'll always be a last twist to the story: Whatever you worship, you imitate; whatever you imitate, you become.

In other words, whatever you value most will ultimately determine who you are.

If you worship money, you'll become greedy at the core of your heart. If you worship some sinful habit, that same sin will grip your soul and poison your character to death. If you worship stuff, your life will become material, void of eternal significance. If you give all your praise to the god of you, you'll become a disappointing little god both to yourself and to all those who trust in you.

Listen to the psalm-writer: "Not to us, O LORD, not to us, but to your name be glory, because of your love and faithfulness." Then comes this observation: "Our God is in heaven, he does whatever pleases him."

Then, by contrast, he supplies this exposé of the idols men make and choose:

> But their idols are silver and gold, made by the hands of men. They have mouths, but cannot speak, eyes, but they cannot see; they have ears, but cannot hear, noses, but they cannot smell; they have hands, but cannot feel, feet, but they cannot walk; nor can they utter a sound with their throats.

Not too high of a score for man-made gods. But here's the clincher:

> Those who make them will be like them, and so will all who trust in them.

Simply put: We become what we worship. If you don't like who you're becoming, take a quick inventory of the things on the throne of your heart.

Chapter 4

WHAT GOD WANTS MOST FOR YOU

God loves you very much. But God also loves Himself, because to do anything less would mean not being God. More than any of us, God knows how valuable He is. He knows He's God. He knows He's central. As a result, He values Himself most.

No, He's not egotistical, thinking more highly of Himself than He should. He's the only God, thinking of Himself as He truly is.

But God's centrality hasn't stopped Him from loving you with the greatest love known to man. And through the death of His Son, God has made a way for you to return to His loving arms, washed clean and forgiven because of the price He paid at the cross of Jesus Christ.

Where your spirit was once dormant because of sin, God seeks to stir your soul to life again, giving you the capacity to walk in intimacy with Him. Restoring your ability to worship with all your heart.

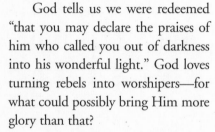

What God wants most for you is for you to have a worthy God.

God tells us we were redeemed "that you may declare the praises of him who called you out of darkness into his wonderful light." God loves turning rebels into worshipers—for what could possibly bring Him more glory than that?

What God wants most for you is for you to have a worthy God. Only then will you live a full and satisfying life.

WHO, NOT WHERE

God doesn't require ornate or elaborate expressions. The worship He's looking for is spiritual and true. Genuine. Authentic. Worship from the heart.

That's how Jesus put it in a conversation He was having with a Samaritan woman one afternoon while resting beside a common well.

Soon into their talk, Jesus was disclosing His knowledge of her private affairs. (After she mentioned that she was unmarried, He pointed out that she'd actually had five husbands, and the man she was now living with wasn't one of them.) That immediately tipped her off that this guy had some kind of special wisdom. She might as well tap into it.

She quickly posed a question that evidently had been bothering her for some time. Her people (the Samaritans) worshiped on one mountain, His people (the Jews) on another. Who was right? Which mountain was better? Where should she worship?

For a total stranger who knew everything about her past, this simple "where" question shouldn't be too hard. Right?

But as we've come to expect, Jesus took the subject to another level, answering a basic "where" question with a riveting "who" answer.

Here's His response:

> Believe me, woman, a time is coming when you will worship the Father neither on this mountain nor in Jerusalem. You Samaritans worship that which you don't know [think UNKNOWN GOD], we worship what we do know, for salvation is from the Jews. Yet a time is coming and now has come when the true worshipers will worship the Father in spirit and truth, for they are the kind of worshipers the Father seeks. God is spirit, and His worshipers must worship in spirit and truth.

Wow!

After that, I'm surprised the woman could gather herself to speak, but she did: "I know that Christ the Messiah is coming and when He comes He will explain everything to us."

(To which I say, "Lady, you're getting very warm!")

But to which Jesus replied, "I who speak to you am He."

Jesus has come. Messiah is here. And He's announcing that worship isn't about where you do it, but about the heart. It's not about what church you belong to, but whether or not you have a personal relationship with God.

The kind of worshipers God is looking for are those who will worship Him as their Father—in spirit and truth.

To worship God *in spirit* requires that we be alive on the inside, experiencing the life He gives by spiritual birth. Without His life, you can never truly worship.

And to worship *in truth* means to worship God as He really is, and bringing more than our words—bringing words amplified by an authentic life that flows from being spiritually alive within.

AWAKEN TO GOD'S INVITATION

But how do you get this inside aliveness? How can we possibly worship in spirit and truth?

Notice how Jesus begins His answer. How He begins God's invitation to a whole new way of worship. Jesus opens with the words, "<u>Believe Me</u>."

For all of us, <u>that's where true worship begins.</u>

This past Sunday at church I was blown away again by the kindness of God. On this particular Sunday it wasn't my pastor's message that got to me, though his message was amazing as always. It wasn't the music. It wasn't even the day's "global theme," though that fueled again my passion for God's glory in all the earth.

No, on this particular Sunday the story for me was a woman singing in a small vocal choir backing up the worship band. We were all standing and worshiping to David Crowder's version of "Make a Joyful Noise," and the place was rocking. As we sang, the camera focused on a woman in the choir named Lori. She was passionately worshiping God with a huge smile that beautifully reflected the joy we were singing about.

As Lori's face filled the big screen, my eyes filled with tears.

I know Lori from 7:22 (a Bible study gathering I'm a part of here in Atlanta). Geared toward young singles, 7:22 draws thousands of them every week to worship from all across our city. Being a middle-aged mom, Lori didn't exactly fit the demographic profile. But her teenage son kept inviting her, and she finally came.

Lori was divorced. She was wounded. And she was spiritually lost.

But she came.

Something about the place made her feel at home. The spirit she sensed among us drew her in. Pretty soon her eyes were opened to the love and grace of God, and on one spring Tuesday night, Lori personally connected with God. Praying a simple prayer, she placed her faith in Christ for eternal life. In an instant she was alive, starting a new journey with God.

Well, that part of the story is amazing enough…but it gets better. It turns out Lori's ex-husband was searching, too. His journey is like so many—a broken childhood and shattered dreams, with deep and desperate wounds leading him down every dead-end road on the planet. In his words, he was "a hard case." A lost cause.

But the transformation happening in Lori's life was too much to ignore, and soon he was opening his heart to the Savior and joining the ranks at 7:22. He, too, became a follower of Christ.

God began to restore the relationship between them, and about a year after Lori became a Christian, they were remarried. Both of them started coming to our church on Sundays, and both were baptized, an expression of their new life in Christ.

A marriage salvaged. Lives restored. A family mended. And two more hearts fully alive to worship the God who made them.

Now here's Lori, in the choir, leading the church to worship the living God!

How could we expect less from God? He's always bringing the dead back to life. Giving the lost unending purpose. Turning rebels into worshipers. Awakening praise from the pits. Putting a song of true worship in our hearts. Allowing us to worship Him as God…and Father.

> God is always turning rebels into worshipers.

It's like David said: "I waited patiently for the LORD; he turned to me and heard my cry. He lifted me…out of the mud and mire; he set my feet on a rock.… He put a new song in my mouth, a hymn of praise to our God."

Watching Lori sing a new song that morning broke my heart with tears of joy.

That's what the power of the gospel is all about.

THE WONDERFUL CROSS

But such a transformation in anyone's life comes at a very high price. God doesn't let us worship Him for free. Our worship cost Him the life of His only Son. Bringing us from death to life required someone besides us paying the ultimate penalty for our sin.

That's why at the center of all true worship stands a

wonderful cross…the cross on which the Son of God died.

But how can that cross be called wonderful? Isn't it a scene of shame? Isn't its beam a place of suffering?

Absolutely. The Roman cross was a cruel and painful ending. It was a place of execution. Rusted nails. Pierced flesh. Gasping breath.

The cross meant humiliation. Judgment. The cross was agony. A place where people hung until breathing and heartbeats ceased.

Jesus experienced the most horrific death imaginable. There's nothing wonderful about how He died. What's wonderful about His cross is *why* He died.

Something truly amazing was happening that day as God offered a ransom for the whole world—Jesus *becoming* sin and shame, suffering and dying for you and me.

To some, it may have appeared that Jesus was being railroaded through the courts of justice and taken by sheer force to die among common criminals. But that's not so.

No one took Jesus' life. He laid it down, willingly satisfying the wrath of a holy God. He chose the cross in order to demonstrate that God was both loving and just. He gave His life so we could receive ours back again. Men may have driven the nails through His hands and feet, but He died because God was sacrificing His only Son.

The cross was the Father's determined end for His Son. The cross was God's idea…God's redemption plan. The cross was the way the door would be opened. The cross was the only way rebels could ever truly worship again.

Yes, it's a blood-stained cross, but a wonderful cross. In fact, it's the most beautiful thing I've ever seen.

The cross of Christ is a cross of healing. A place of unconditional love. A place of sweet embrace. From His cross rings salvation's song, declaring to all that redemption has come. From it flows forgiveness free. The cross of Christ is a place of peace.

> The cross of Christ is where true worship begins.

And the place where true worship begins.

In fact, even as Jesus was dying, worship was very near.

Remember the story? A Roman centurion was standing there, doing his job while Jesus breathed His last breath. As Jesus died, the heavens rumbled and darkened, and the earth shook with awe. All of creation shuddered at the sight.

Then, witnessing the greatest act of mercy history has ever known, this Roman soldier—who with his companions had stripped, beaten, mocked, and crucified Jesus—was compelled to proclaim, "Truly this man was the Son of God."

Amazing! This supposed enemy of Christ was the first

of many to have his eyes opened to God's redemption story. He was the first among us to see the wonder of it all.

And in a heartbeat, right there in the midst of the stench and sorrow, worship began at the foot of the cross.

Chapter 5

JOINING THE RANKS OF TRUE WORSHIPERS

My hope is that somewhere in the pages of this book you'll find yourself moving closer and closer to those whom Jesus calls "true worshipers," those who worship the Father from the heart with all they are…with all they have.

You may be like the woman Jesus met by the well that day—more concerned with your "place" of worship than the God you meet there.

Or you may be like Lori once was, feeling far away from the love of God.

You might be just waking up to the idea of worship in the first place, only now realizing it's that thing you've been doing your whole life long. Only now sensing you need to redirect its flow.

Or maybe you're a passionate lover of God, but frustrated by the presence of little idols you've kept around far too long.

For all of us, the time for true worship is now. The door is open. The price has been paid. Jesus is here.

Making the Move

So while the whole world is busy glorifying who knows what, God is inviting any and all to join the ranks of the true worshipers—those who are beginning to discover the connection between His infinite worth and their own longing within to love something supremely.

We began this book by seeing that worship is our response to what we value most. That's the basic, entry-level definition, describing the kind of worship everybody does all the time. Not unlike Webster defining worship as "extreme devotion or intense love or admiration of any kind."

But now we're going deeper. Now we're making the move from worshiping any god that dangles in our view to responding to the invitation of the matchless God of gods. Now we're talking about a brand of worship that's lasting and true. The kind we were made for. Worship that both honors God and satisfies us.

For this we need a bigger definition, one that will take us deeper as we move together toward a life of true worship.

Here we go—

Worship is…
our response,
both personal and corporate,
to God—
for who He is!
and what He has done!
expressed in and by the things we say
and the way we live.

Granted, it's not real catchy and concise. But then again, we're not taking on a tiny subject. The definition may be a mouthful, but I like it. And as I dig down to uncover its meaning, it puts a lot of skin on the bones.

In a nutshell, it's saying true worship is a whole-life response to God's greatness and glory.

It's Something You Do

Worship is a verb—at least that's what author Robert Webber says in his book by the same title.

I think he's right. Practically speaking, worship is always a verb. Worship is something you do.

Worship isn't something you *watch,* contrary to the thinking of many of us who attend church. That may be hard to believe, given that in most churches the rows of seats (or pews) are arranged with sight lines in mind. The lights also point to the stage. And to help you with your viewing pleasure, you're handed a program at the door—a lineup card for what's happening up front in today's "show," if you will. After all, it's all put on for you, is it not?

Worship is something you do. It isn't something you watch.

But here's a news flash for you. Worship isn't something you attend, like a film or a concert. Worship is something you enter into with all your might. Worship is a participation activity in a spectator culture.

Check out the Psalms, both the longest book in the entire Bible and the one that deals almost exclusively with the subject of worship. The Psalms are filled with verbs:

Shout to God. Sing a new song. Dance before Him. Clap your hands. Bow down. Lift up your heads. Tell of His might. Stand in awe. Meditate on His truth. Walk in His ways. Still your heart. Cast down your idols. Run to Him. Make a loud noise. Lift your hands. Strike up the band (okay, so that one's a bit modernized). Clash the cymbals. Praise Him with trumpet sound. Seek His face. Tell the nations.

True worship is a whole-life response to God's greatness and glory. A response that taps our mind, our soul, our heart of passion…and all our strength.

IT DOESN'T START WITH US

I think the key word in our new definition is *response.*

Worship is our response to God. In other words, we don't initiate worship; God does.

He reveals; we respond.

He discloses; we respond.

He unveils; we respond.

He chooses to show us how amazing He is; we say, "God, You're amazing!"

Our whole relationship with God works the same way:

He loves. We love in return.

He calls. We answer.

He leads. We follow.

IF ONLY YOU WERE THERE

Several years ago Shelley and I were at a youth camp in Texas, hanging out one afternoon by the senior high pool. (Yes, they had their own pool; middle schoolers once again get the raw end of the deal!) About fifty students stood in the shallow end while four or five of their friends were putting on a diving exhibition at the other.

This camp's pool still had a high dive (one of few still

remaining in our litigious era). And the brave few were taking their turns entertaining the rest. I remember two of them as if I were sitting there now.

One was quite together. Must have been a gymnast—he was ripped and fit, with perfect "pool hair" and even better form. A typical dive for him would begin with the "Olympic pause" on the very last fraction of the board, continuing with various twists and tucks and turns. Like a missile he would knife into the water, then quickly swim to the side and lean back and shake his wonderful hair as he nonchalantly swaggered back to the ladder.

He was cocky. But he was good.

But another guy was stealing the show. He couldn't dive like "pretty boy" if he had to, but that hardly mattered.

He was robust, full of life, a tad heavy, and sporting yellow surf shorts that hung well below his knees. After each of Mr. Wonderful's successive attempts, this guy would appear. Not too bright, but fearless nonetheless, he would fly off the board like mad.

Can you see him? On this particular turn, the yellow shorts guy is doing a "watermelon" from fifteen feet up, proceeding to splash everyone in the shallow end of the pool.

Everybody's laughing. Everyone's smiling. He's making the afternoon a lot of fun at the senior pool.

But on his next attempt, things turn ugly. Fast.

This time he's flying off into the air with a little extra

boost, but it quickly becomes apparent to all that he hasn't exactly thought through this maneuver before leaving the diving board.

Soon he's in midflight, perpendicular with the water, no more revolutions to take place, and coming down. Face up and stretched out, he has lost the battle with gravity—and the pool is getting closer by the second.

At this point I turned my attention to the audience in the shallow end of the pool. By the expressions on their faces, I could tell something awful was about to happen. Their eyes were getting wider and wider. An eerie quiet settled over the entire pool.

Then I heard it: SPLAT! You've heard it before—the horrible sound of human flesh solidly smacking the water.

At once—as if somehow the minds of everyone watching had been melded into one—a groan emerged from deep inside each person: *UUHHHhhhhhhh!*

It was one of the most concerted things I've ever seen teenagers do.

It was if they were being led, almost like someone had been calling a play-by-play commentary then orchestrating their response: "Okay, everyone, he's coming down! He's at ten feet and dropping like lead—eight feet, I'm thinking ugly—four, get ready to groan—three, he's gonna hit hard—two, it's going to be a back-buster—one—let's hear it all together…NOW!"

UUHHHhhhhhhh!

But there was no director there that day telling the students what to do and when to do it. What they did was natural, the most appropriate response to what they were seeing. It was spontaneous. True.

And no matter how vividly I try to describe what happened on that summer afternoon, I couldn't possibly get you to respond with the same agony and intensity that they did. Sure, you may cringe a little just hearing about it; but to respond as they did in that moment, you had to have seen what they were seeing.

> Worship is what spontaneously flows out of us when we come face-to-face with Him.

LOOK UP

The same thing that was true in the pool that afternoon is true of our worship today. Unless we see God, we cannot worship Him. Worship is what spontaneously flows out of us when we come face-to-face with Him. It's the natural response to all of who He is. Our uncalculated response for all He has done.

Sure, we get a massive amount out of the experience of worshiping Him. But at its core, worship is all about God. It's *for* Him. Our worship is *to* Him.

That's why we say—

Worship is…
our response,
both personal and corporate,
to God—
for who He is!
and what He has done!

So often in the Psalms we find expressions very similar to this one: "Great is the LORD and greatly to be praised." When you boil it all down, true worship is simply catching sight of the greatness, majesty, splendor, glory, and grace of an infinite God.

When God is not greatly praised, it's only because we don't think He's that great of a God. When our worship is small, it's because our concept of God is small. When we offer God little-bitty sacrifices, it's because we've somehow reduced Him in our hearts to a little-bitty God. Our vision has become clouded, our hearts distracted.

As a result, our lives shrivel into insignificance and meaninglessness. We just bump along in this mass of humanity, having no real clue what life's all about. We fret. We get depressed. We worry and get bent out of shape. We go down all kinds of dead-end paths as we try to accomplish everything by ourselves.

We lose sight of the reality of all realities: There's an

infinite, limitless God high and exalted on His throne, ruling with all power and authority over the heavens and the earth. A God who's still running the show—running our lives and running the whole universe on His timetable.

And at this very moment, while He holds entire galaxies in place by His power, He also invites us at any time day or night to look up and behold Him as He is.

Chapter 6

FOR WHO HE IS, FOR WHAT HE DOES

How can we recover a more exalted view of God in our lives? How can we become the true worshipers we were designed to be? How can we bring back into focus a sense of how awesome God is?

The answer is, we can't. Not on our own, that is. Unless God Himself shows us who He is, we can't respond to Him with true worship from our hearts.

God reveals…so we can respond. In authentic, natural worship.

So what is He showing us? If authentic worship is the natural response to what God has revealed…then what exactly has He revealed about Himself?

Well, this book, and ten thousand like it, could never contain the sum total of His greatness and worth. There's no way we could grasp it all.

But there's so much we *can* know. Enough, in fact, to keep us praising for a lifetime.

For now, let's just think about two facets of His character that reveal His heart to you and me.

INFINITELY AWESOME

We know God is infinitely awesome.

This God with whom we deal is no small fry. He's not our size. Not even somewhat larger. He's not made of the stuff we're made of. He doesn't have to deal with our barriers and limitations.

> We don't really even know what "infinite" is all about.

"Before the mountains were born, or You gave birth to the earth and the world, even from everlasting to everlasting, You are God." Notice that the psalmist didn't write, "from everlasting to everlasting You *were* God." But, You *are* God.

What does it mean that God is infinite? Simply that He *is*. Beyond that, our little brains are hard pressed for more. We don't really even know what "infinite" is all about. Try to define it. Infinite means having no limits. Never running out. Having no end. Existing forever. Unbound. Timeless. Stuff we can't fully comprehend.

God has never been tired. Never slept. Never aged. Never upgraded.

He's self-sufficient. Self-contained. God doesn't need anything. Or anybody.

If all of us happen to fall off the face of the earth, God will still be exactly who He is. If all of us abandon our worship of Him, He'll remain the same. God's greatness doesn't depend on us. If not one single person on earth ever chose to respond to Him in love, believing in Him and worshiping Him, God would still be all that He already is, always has been, and always will be.

> Oh, the depth of the riches both of the wisdom and knowledge of God! How unsearchable are His judgments and unfathomable His ways!
>
> Who has known the mind of the Lord? Or who has been his counselor? Who has ever given to God, that God should repay him? For from him and through him and to him are all things. To him be the glory forever! Amen.

Science is gaining ground everyday. We can look farther into space and deeper within our bodies than ever before. And what we discover stuns and amazes us. We're finding there's more out in space than we ever imagine. And more complexity within than we can understand.

We've put men on the moon, but we can't quite make it to Mars, our closest planet neighbor. We inhabit a galaxy comprised of billions of stars, of which our mighty sun is average at best. And our Milky Way is only one galaxy among billions more, each housing billions of other stars.

We'll never see more than the tiniest fraction of them. Yet God has given each one a name:

> Lift your eyes and look to the heavens: Who cre-
> ated all these? He Who brings out the starry host
> one by one, and calls them each by name. Because
> of His great power and mighty strength, not one
> of them is missing.

And while we wrestle with the cause of it all, He offers this simple, yet irrefutable explanation: "In the beginning God created the heavens and the earth." And why not? If you're as awesome as He is, why not make a universe that's vast enough to constantly echo your greatness back to you?

But, more than just making the universe for His glory, God did it to show Himself to you and me. "For since the creation of the world God's invisible qualities—his eternal power and divine nature—have been clearly seen, being understood from what has been made, so that men are without excuse."

Using the adjective *awesome* has become common in the conversations of our day. But nothing is really awesome but God alone.

God is awesome in glory. And awesome in holiness. On more than one occasion we glimpse into heaven and hear the angels repeating, "Holy, holy, holy is the Lord Almighty." In fact, holiness is the only one of His attributes that we see angels repeating over and over again. Is it possible that holiness is at the heart of God's God-ness? The center of all of who He is?

When you're God, you're always who you are.

God is pure. Radiant. Without blemish or stain. He is untainted goodness. Without fault or blame. Perfection personified.

When you're God, you're always who you are—unchanging, unaffected by anything or anyone.

INTIMATELY APPROACHABLE

And if God's infinite nature isn't mind-boggling enough, consider this: The infinitely awesome God is inviting you to draw near Him.

Who is like the LORD our God, who is enthroned on high, who humbles Himself to behold the things that are in heaven and in the earth?

Yes, He's enthroned on high, but God has lowered Himself to take notice of our lives. To become, as David said, "intimately acquainted" with all our ways.

Think about it. This great and majestic God is totally aware of every single detail of your life. He's God in heaven, yet He knows everything there is to know about you, things you don't even know about yourself.

What a miraculous thing that we're invited to respond to this incredible God. That the Almighty One has somehow chosen of His own free will to desire your worship. Though He had no real need or obligation to do so, He invites you near to be His true worshiper.

How can it be that God is infinite in being and power, yet you and I can touch Him? We can touch His heart. We can cause joy to come to Him. Cause Him to smile. We can bring God pleasure.

Your worship matters to God.

It's true that "the heavens are telling of the glory of God." But right where you are in this moment, God is there and He's saying, "I want you to tell of My glory, too."

The rocks He has made are capable of singing songs, should He ask them to; but He draws near your side and whispers, "I'd rather hear *you* sing a new song of praise to Me!"

God is constantly surrounded by heavenly throngs and endless praise, yet He says to you and me, "I know your voice, even the thoughts of your heart. And your arrows of affection reach My heart."

ALWAYS HANGING IN THE BALANCE

Infinitely awesome—intimately approachable.

Creator—Father.

Lord Almighty—friend.

A contradiction? No. A paradox? For sure.

That God is both of these at once is part of His divine mystery—something we're better off not trying to figure out. Instead, we need only embrace the mystery, holding on to what my friend refers to so often as "the friendship and the fear."

If we're going to worship God for who He is, we have to continually live in the tension of these two aspects of His character. If we swing too far to the "approachable" end of the spectrum, we'll eventually reduce God to someone our own size.

By doing so, we'll dishonor Him and forget who we are. Soon we'll be frustrated by this little god we've made for ourselves. Our worship will shrink like socks in a dryer. And our faith will diminish, robbing us of hope and robbing God of His glory.

But we cannot forgo His invitation to intimacy, either. How can we forget that through the wonder of grace we belong to Him as sons and daughters? We are the loved children of God. We get no extra credit in heaven for keeping Him at arm's length. Especially given the fact He has bulldozed His way through the wall of sin and shame that kept us from Him.

We are His, filled with His Spirit. And His Spirit cries out from within our hearts, "Abba, Father." So we consider how awesome He is, standing in awe of all He has done—and at the same time we boldly embrace Him through the life of His Son, loving Him tenderly like a child in his daddy's hug.

AND IF THAT'S NOT REASON ENOUGH

Our worship begins with our response to who God is. But that's not all we have to be thankful for. That's not all we have to celebrate.

Don't get me wrong. If all you ever know about God is what you know right now, you still know enough to praise Him forever.

But there's more.

In addition to God's infinite character, we praise Him for everything He's done.

> Worship is…
> our response,
> both personal and corporate,
> to God—
> for who He is!
> and *what He has done!*

It's the potent combination of these two areas of praise that causes worship to always be an option for us, no matter what.

When we can't tell what God is up to, and we can't see Him working around in our circumstances, we can still praise Him simply for who we know Him to be. Even if our circumstances don't reveal it, God is still all of who He is. No matter what life sends our way, we focus our attention on Him. He's still God.

In that same way, we can always praise Him for what He has done, though at times we feel we can't quite sense that He is near.

Our lives are filled with gifts from God, little miracles. The trees that line the road we take to work. The car (new or not so new) that gets us there. A chance to work. Eyes to see. A place to sleep. His faithfulness in days gone by. All these should keep us worshiping moment by moment. Let's face it, gratitude for the gift of breath alone should keep us praising for quite some time!

We praise God for who He is.

We honor Him for all He has done.

Even if God never does another thing for us, should we cease to praise? Of course not—not when we remember all that He's already done through the gift of His Son.

WORSHIP AS A
WAY OF LIFE

Which would you prefer?

— A husband who tells you he loves you ten times a day...or one who's faithful to you alone, consistently doing the things that show he cares?

— A significant other who gives you homemade cards with "you're-the-best-thing-in-my life" messages...or one who respects you, honors you, and doesn't date around on you?

— Kids who tell you how much you mean to them...or kids who are trustworthy, caring enough to obey you because they believe you want their very best?

— Friends who keep reminding you that you're their best friend...or those who are there when you need them most, never stabbing you in the back when you're not around?

If you're like me, your answer is…BOTH! I want the words *and* the actions. I'm guessing the same can be said about you.

Well, God is no different. The worship He's after is a BOTH kind of worship.

I think that's why there are two primary words for worship in the New Testament. Each having a different, but important, meaning.

Jesus used one of them in His conversation with the Samaritan woman beside the well. This word is all about an attitude of honor and reverence. It means literally "to bow before," or "to kiss the hand of a king."

The other word has a much less glamorous meaning. It simply means to serve.

It's the word Paul uses in a pivotal passage on worship. He begins by "beseeching" us—begging us—"in view of God's mercy, to offer your bodies as living sacrifices, holy and pleasing to God." This, Paul declares, is our "spiritual act of worship." Or literally, our spiritual "service."

Paul was saying, If you've seen mercy…if you've seen the cross…then offer all of who you are in response to all that He has done.

Let's face it: That kind of full-blown serving is not real

high on our priority list. But in the mind of God, worship = serving. Worship = life.

What We Can Do

What God has revealed to us about Himself is beyond our words of gratitude. What He has done on our behalf makes it impossible for us to ever repay Him.

But what we *can* do in return—and must do—is give Him everything we have through a life of service to Him and to those around us.

That's what we mean when we say worship is a way of life.

For far too long, people have been cheating God, somehow thinking that if they just keep telling Him He's great, He'll be content. Whether their words are genuine doesn't seem to matter. Whether their lives back up their words is no big deal.

After all, words come so easy. And saying (and singing) them makes us feel a little better about ourselves.

But God isn't honored by words alone. Like any of us, He's moved by words that are authenticated by actions. When it comes to worship, it's the total package that matters—what you say, how you say it, and whether you mean it. And our words mean most when they're amplified in every area of our lives.

> Worship is…
> our response,
> both personal and corporate,
> to God —
> for who He is!
> and what He has done!
> expressed in and by *the things we say
> and the way we live.*

On Sunday morning you may be singing with all you've got, maybe even falling on your knees to tell God He's your "all in all." But the whole time He may be thinking, *There seem to be a lot of other things in your life lately that you desire a whole lot more than Me.*

In that moment, we're no different from those of ages past about whom God said, "These people honor me with their lips, but their hearts are far from me."

God knows how inclined we are to say one thing and do another. That's why the true test of worship isn't so much what we say, but how we live.

How Can We Offer Less?

God has given us "life and breath and all things," as Paul told those guys in Athens. The only fitting response to all He has done is to give back to Him all that we are. Anything less is not enough. Anything less is not true worship. Anything less only proves that we haven't really seen Him at all.

Take, for instance, His mercy and grace.

We deserved death, but received life. God's grace and mercy are really just that simple.

So how do we respond to the cross of Christ?

With a Sunday visit to the church down the street?

By dropping two bucks in the offering plate?

Singing a few verses of a trusted hymn?

Offering a brief prayer of grace over the Thanksgiving turkey?

Wearing a cross?

Owning a Bible?

Praying for a missionary once in a while?

> God knows how inclined we are to say one thing and do another.

No way! The only right response to such mercy and grace is our *everything*.

I'm the Offering

Somewhere in the modern culture we've become confused, thinking that worship and songs are one and the same.

The church scene is awash in new worship songs. That's not a bad thing in and of itself. But it's deadly when we make a subtle mental shift and start believing that by singing the songs, we're worshiping in truth.

Don't get me wrong. I'm all for songs of worship—both old and new.

We've become confused, thinking that worship and songs are one and the same.

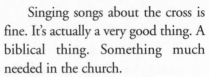

Singing songs about the cross is fine. It's actually a very good thing. A biblical thing. Something much needed in the church.

But a song alone is not enough. The cross demands more.

Grace requires that we bring ourselves, laying our lives before this merciful God.

This wholehearted, full-on, life-encompassing response to God's amazing grace is the "reasonable" thing to do, as one translation expresses it in that pivotal worship passage from Paul.

Giving God everything is our only reasonable response.

Now, check out Paul's challenging words again, this time from a contemporary paraphrase:

> So here's what I want you to do, God helping you:
> Take your everyday, ordinary life—your sleeping,
> eating, going-to-work, and walking-around life—
> and place it before God as an offering. Embracing

what God does for you is the best thing you can do for Him.

That's it! Worshiping God is what we do as we respond to His mercy in our "walking-around life."

It's not the words I sing, but me I bring;
    I'm the offering laid at Your feet,
My steps the melody, oh so sweet,
    All of me in praise of Thee.

Chapter 8

THROUGH JESUS, ALL THE TIME

As I've continued over the years to try to grasp the fullness of what worship is about, this passage of Scripture has consistently captured my attention:

> Through Him then, let us continually offer up a sacrifice of praise to God, that is, the fruit of lips that give thanks to His name. And do not neglect doing good and sharing, for with such sacrifices God is pleased.

We know from the context of the surrounding verses that the "Him" in the first phrase refers to Jesus.

I believe the meaning hits us more forcefully when His name is included in the text:

Through Jesus then, let us continually offer a sacrifice of praise to God....

Jesus is the everlasting door by which we come to worship God.

No More Religious Systems

We're no longer under any religious system. Not that of the Old Testament, or any other. In the past, God-worshipers had to approach Him through a ritualistic system of sacrifice. But not anymore.

> We're no longer under any religious system.

Christ is the final offering for sin; He offered "one sacrifice for sins for all time." So as we come to worship the Father, we aren't required to bring a sacrifice in an attempt to make us right with God. Jesus has already done that for us.

This truth is important to grasp because we consistently fail to live as we should live. And when we fail, the enemy is quick to condemn us, telling us we can't possibly be a worshiper after what we've done.

But those words are lies. We can always come back to God in worship, no matter where we've been or how far we've fallen.

How can that be?

Through Jesus Christ. His death has made it possible for us to be accepted by God. His cross has made our worship acceptable in the Father's sight. We can approach His throne of grace. Anytime. Anywhere.

That's why a deep awareness of the cross is almost always in my mind as I come to worship. And if it's not, the Holy Spirit puts it there. Fast.

NAIL OPEN THE DOOR

How can I embrace this awesome God of wonder and not cherish the cross that allows me to approach Him at all?

So many people don't know the fullness of what Christ has done for them. The greatness of who He has made them to be. They don't know enough about their new standing with God in Christ to break free from the lies of the deceiver.

They try to worship, but condemnation abounds. Guilt restrains. Shame stifles.

No wonder their worship is weak and lame. No wonder there aren't too many among us shouting His praise or breaking out in a dance of unrestrained celebration.

Maybe we're not getting the gospel—the whole gospel.

In Jesus Christ we're free! We are eternally forgiven. Washed clean. Made new. Re-created.

There's no more condemnation for anyone in Christ

Jesus. He's our life. His righteousness is our righteousness. We're born again. Children of God. Permanently attached to Him. Our debt is paid in full. Sin's power is broken. Death is defeated. We're alive!

These are the truths that nail open the doorway into God's presence. And you, too, can come through that door to worship. Not because of you. But because of the cross.

YOU CAN'T BE SERIOUS

We always come to worship through the doorway of Jesus Christ. But check out what comes next in that Hebrews passage: "Through Jesus then, let us continually offer a sacrifice of praise to God."

Hello! Are you seeing what I'm seeing?

Continually!

God's got to be kidding, right?

Continually offer Him a sacrifice of praise? Like 24/7? Day and night? All the time? How is that even possible?

Maybe we should all join a monastery after all. Or maybe we should just take a deep breath and consider what the writer of these verses is suggesting.

For one, he's making a massive

> These are the truths that nail open the doorway into God's presence.

point with his first-century readers who were quite familiar with the smells and sights of animal sacrifices. They knew what it meant to come once a week or once a year, bringing some animal as an offering to God.

But it's not like that anymore. We're not talking about a once-a-week or twice-a-year thing. We're talking about a new relationship that allows us to praise God at any moment, in any setting. On the freeway. In a restaurant. In our dorm room. On a soccer field. In a boardroom.

Continually means that any time is the right time to praise God!

ADJUSTMENT TIME

And *continually* means a huge attitude adjustment is in order. *Continually* means that in every moment we're looking for ways to glorify Him.

Continually gets our worship outside the walls of the church building.

Continually gets our worship outside of our devotional times.

Continually gets worship outside of our Christian conferences.

Our worship events.
Our MP3 players.
Our headphones.
Continually gets worship into the marketplace.

Into our hangout places.

Into our conversations with friends.

Into our Starbucks moments.

Continually gets worship into our entertainment choices.

Our bank accounts.

Our hidden thoughts.

Our dark nights.

Our joys.

What God is saying is this: "Everything you are—is Me. Everything you have—is Mine. The life you live is My life that I've freely given you. And I want worshipers who will constantly reflect My goodness and grace with that life."

God wants our lives to be a seamless cord of worship. God wants our worship to be a way of life.

Chapter 9

FROM OUR LIPS
AND FROM
OUR LIVES

Our continual sacrifice of praise—our all-the-time expression of worship to God—takes two primary shapes.

It's made up of words. And deeds.

Let's look again at that Hebrews passage and see where it takes us:

> Through Jesus then, let us continually offer a sacrifice of praise to God, that is, the fruit of lips that give thanks to His name. And do not neglect doing good and sharing with others, for with such sacrifices God is pleased.

The first part of continual praise is the "fruit of our lips," which magnify God. That phrase "the fruit of our lips" may sound a little odd, but I like it.

There's no fruit without some kind of root. So whatever comes out of my mouth actually comes from the roots that have taken hold deep in my soul. That's why Scripture says that what comes out of the mouth is actually coming from the heart.

My praise to God doesn't just roll off my lips, but begins deep down inside me. (Very cool concept!)

God is looking for the kind of people who are always soaking in His Word, sinking the roots of His character into their minds and hearts. As a result, true and kind expressions to and about Him are constantly coming out of their mouths.

I think that's what David means when he says, "I will bless the LORD at all times; His praise will continually be in my mouth."

ACTIONS THAT EXPRESS

But verbal praise isn't the only kind of worship God is into. The passage goes on to expand worship to include acts of compassion and integrity, sacrifices that really make God happy.

Now we're moving beyond the fruit of our lips and talking about the fruit of our lives.

And the same principle applies: If we immerse ourselves in God's character, God's character starts to grow "on the limbs of our tree." His character will eventually find expression in the things we do.

When we do the right thing, God is worshiped. Even if no one notices or cares. God's truth is reflected back to Him. Even if we're penalized for our honesty, God is honored by our sacrifice.

> When we do the right thing, God is worshiped.

And when we care for someone else, the passage reminds us, then "God is pleased."

It's a lot easier to sing a song than it is to stop and touch the broken. It's a lot less taxing to go to church than to take "church" to the world. But sharing with others is a sacrifice of worship that makes God smile.

WHAT IT CAN LOOK LIKE

I have a friend living in Afghanistan. He's been there for several years, working among some of the most desperate people on earth. Years of war, famine, and evil regimes have reduced their lives to what they wear on their backs.

Men, women, and children—displaced within their own country. No jobs. No home. No shelter. Little future.

My friend is bright. Educated. And a believer in God.

John could live anywhere in America. But he doesn't.

Having abandoned the American dream for greater riches, he can be found most days in some Afghan village…overseeing a relief project, establishing an educational training center, or monitoring a food distribution program.

He's loving people and meeting their needs. And when they ask why, John smiles a smile rooted deep down in the grace of God, and he tells them about Jesus Christ.

He is more than a missionary. He's a worshiper in spirit and truth. A worshiper in action and deed.

What do you think moves God more? Our singing "Shout to the north and the south, sing to the east and the west, Jesus is Savior to all, Lord of heaven and earth" a hundred more times?

Or one undignified worshiper walking the streets of Afghanistan, touching the world's "least" in Jesus' name.

If you've been playing along, you know by now the answer is BOTH.

The song has a place in the worship of the church, spurring us on in God's mission of mercy to the world. But at some point we've got to live the song, being willing to go to people everywhere who are waiting to hear about a grace that's free.

God loves the world. Every soul in it. He wants all nations to know His name. All people to taste His goodness. Every heart to sing His praise.

But those who have not yet heard of this seeking God will never awaken to worship in truth until we do. Until we worship with our words and our lives. Until we reflect His wonder and grace in every corner of the world.

Making the Mundane a Melody

Sure, you're thinking, *going to Afghanistan is a wonderful thing. But I work in the drive-through at the bank.*

I understand. Most people do.

No, I don't mean they work at a bank drive-through. But most people find themselves in places that don't seem all that spiritual. Or worshipful. Jobs that seem pointless apart from paying the bills or filling the time. Circumstances that don't appear to have any eternal significance at all.

If you've ever felt like that, I've got great news. You can worship God wherever you are...doing whatever it is you do!

> Your attitude of worship can turn any mundane task into an offering to God.

That's the beautiful thing about continual praise. Your attitude of worship can turn any mundane task into an offering to God.

Worship can even happen at the photocopier.

It did for me.

As a college student in Atlanta, I worked part-time at the Centers for Disease Control. Pretty impressive, huh? There I was stemming the spread of infectious diseases, developing groundbreaking technologies to improve human life and alleviate suffering!

Well…not exactly.

To be precise, I was the photocopy boy in the Centers' medical library. My main function was making photocopies of the hundreds of articles that various doctors wanted for their personal use.

I didn't exactly have an office—more of a cubbyhole. The photocopier was in a four-by-eight-foot room beneath a stairway at the back of the library. The slanted ceiling dropped below head height on one side. The room overflowed with carts loaded with medical journals waiting to be copied, each having white slips of paper sticking out of them, telling me what to do next.

Hour after hour after hour it was just me and that machine. Day after day the requests piled up.

Working, Worshiping

But God was doing a lot in my heart in those days, and the job for me became something more. I'm not trying to over-spiritualize what happened (we didn't end up having a revival in the library), but by God's grace I was able to turn that copy room into a place I loved.

For one thing, I wanted to be the best copier on earth, never leaving work until every waiting article was reproduced…something that often required improvements in my technique, speed, and productivity. I would not be denied.

But also, this job gave me lots of time to hang out with God. Photocopying, though manually intensive, doesn't overly deplete the brain. That left lots of time for thoughts of God. Time to talk to Him. Time to worship. Time to listen. Time to pray.

Everyone working there knew I was a believer, but they weren't exactly asking me to lead a Bible study or talk about the Savior. My witness was my work…and my worship. Maybe even more significant than anything else I could do or say.

> Everything on earth (except sin) can be done as an act of worship to God.

I became, to put it modestly, the master copier. And you know what? I think the way I did my work reflected something good about the character of God.

When I left, it took three new employees to match my pace! And who knows—one of those articles might have contributed to the untangling of some global disease. (For that, you can thank me later!)

The point is this: Everything on earth (except sin) can be

done as an act of worship to God. Everything we do *is* worship when we do it for Him, displaying His face as we go.

The question is not *what* you do, but *who* you do it for.

Your calling is to turn your place in life into a place of true worship.

To do whatever you do in a way that will reflect God's heart to those around you.

It's to worship…as you live your life.

Chapter 10

A PERSONAL PATH TO WORSHIP

Developing a personal life of worship is the most important thing you can do. It's where the worship journey begins.

We've talked a lot about our worship being a response to God. If that's so, we've got to keep Him in view, daily pursuing the process of discovering who He is.

For some, I know, that's an intimidating task.

Get to know God? you wonder. *Where would I even start?*

Slowly. Simply.

You take one step at a time.

BIG THINGS, IN SMALL PIECES

The first (and so far only!) real mountain I've climbed is the Matterhorn. No, not the one at Disney. The nearly 15,000-foot version in the Alps; a sheer triangle of snow-covered rock looming above the pristine little village of Zermatt, Switzerland.

Though at home I'd trained like crazy in the summer heat, I hadn't taken the time to actually learn about the mountain itself. I'd never even seen a picture of the mountain before. My friend and fellow climber, Marc, had assured me it was doable. That's all I needed to know.

When we arrived in Zermatt, what I saw at the valley's end was an intimidating peak of stone. The two angled sides facing the village seemed to rise straight up to a narrow ridgeline at the top. Certainly no one was going up that way!

At first sight of it, I said to my wife, Shelley, "Don't worry; our way up must be on the back side. There's no way we're climbing that!"

Well, to make a really long and death-defying story manageable, we did. We climbed right up that imposing face!

This was more mountain than I bargained for, and I was quickly aware of the fact that I hadn't trained hard enough. I instantly wished I'd done a little investigating before we arrived. Yet, had I done so, we most likely wouldn't have arrived at all!

In fact, on the main Matterhorn web page, which I didn't check out until we were safely home, is the injunction, "Inexperienced climbers should not attempt an ascent of Matterhorn as their first mountain." As it turns out, the Matterhorn is one of Europe's toughest climbs, with one of the highest death rates for climbers. It wasn't scaled until 1865—the last of the Alps to surrender to exploration.

On the night before our scheduled sprint to the summit, Marc and I tried to sleep at a place called the *Hörnlihütte,* 3,654 feet below the mountain's peak.

Honestly, I had my doubts about the climb.

But we set out for the top in the early morning darkness—along with our two Swiss guides—and were soon going straight up what seemed like mile-high slabs of unconquerable granite. We climbed for the most part on our hands and feet. And we did it in little chunks—constantly moving, yet only a few feet at a time.

At last, we stood on the eighteen-inch-wide summit of this mountaineering jewel. I wept with tears of both relief and amazement. Even more impressive, we made it back down again, an achievement that I now know is far more demanding (and important) than getting to the top. But that's another story.

CLIMBING MOUNT GOD

So—how do you scale something as majestic as Mount God?

A little at a time.

A good place to begin is by getting a Bible and a blank journal, and carving out a few quiet minutes every day for a month. If you need a name for the journey, call it Thirty Days of Praise.

Before you begin each day, breathe this simple prayer to God: "Father, I'm here for You. Please show me who You are."

> Breathe this simple prayer to God: "Father, I'm here for You. Please show me who You are."

Open to the Psalms and begin to read. The goal here is quality, not quantity. You may be content with a verse or two, or you may want to focus on a whole psalm. But don't speed along. Let the words sink in.

As you read, look for one attribute of God that seems to grab your attention. An attribute is simply something that's true about God. A part of His character. A facet of His heart. One of His names.

Maybe you'll be drawn to His mercy. Or His consistency. His love. His holiness.

Maybe your heart will zero in on the fact that He's your Sustainer. Shepherd. Shelter. Friend.

When you feel like one thing has captured your heart, write that attribute on the top of your journal page. You might want to write the verse down, too.

Now take some time to meditate on that aspect of God's character. For example, think about what it means that God is wise. That He embodies "all the treasures of wisdom and knowledge." And think about what God's wisdom means to your life today.

After a few minutes, write your thoughts to God. You might write your own psalm of praise back to Him, or just a stream of thoughts as they spill over from your heart to His.

You might write a new song, or just sing one you already know that magnifies the dimension of His heart that you're focusing on.

You might want to draw. Or diagram. Whatever interprets what's on the inside of your soul. Whatever expresses your response to God.

Make it personal. Intimate. Honest.

Remember, there's no right or wrong way to journal your response to what you see of Him. Two sentences can be as powerful as two pages.

Now carry that word with you all day long. Keep the conversation with God going everywhere you go.

You might be surprised how many times that characteristic appears as you walk through your day.

Every time it does, thank Him for the truth He has

shown you. Praise Him for who He is.

After thirty days, you'll be encouraged at how far along you are on the path of knowing Him. And you'll be amazed at how much more there is of Him to search out.

GETTING CLOSER IS THE KEY

I don't guess you'd be too surprised to know I have a huge print of the Matterhorn hanging on my office wall. And a large edition, coffee-table book about the mountain is at the house. More than one unsuspecting visitor to our home has been subjected to my tales about the climb, as section by section this book records the very route of our ascent in full-page photos that take your breath away.

> You'll be encouraged at how far along you are on the path of knowing Him.

When I first picked up the book in a shop in Zermatt, I was totally unnerved by the immensity of the images. Then, as I looked more closely at what I first thought were shots of the mountain alone, I could see antlike men, climbers within the rocks. Barely visible dots making their way slowly up the mountain. The closer I looked, the more I found.

"Over there, three more. And look right here, six more going up."

I discovered this giant rock is a little deceiving. From a distance the Matterhorn looks smooth and sheer. But once you actually get on the mountain you discover it's jagged. Full of cracks and crevices. Little places to get a foothold or a toehold as you make your way to the peak.

In the same way, there are endless crevices in the character of God. When we break His Word into little chunks, we find a lot of places to settle. Hidden places, offering good footing as we seek to know Him more.

Recently I was looking back at my first worship journal, the one I began in the summer of 1984.

On Thursday, July 26, my underlined word for the day is *Unsearchable*. Beneath it are these words:

> Great is the LORD and highly to be praised; His greatness is unsearchable.
>
> PSALM 145:3

Unsearchable…does that cause us to feel frustrated and give up?

I think, rather, it calls out to something within us, calling us to come to the beauty of the Lord. There's plenty for all—at all times.

I cannot exhaust God. His praise, however, will exhaust this life of mine as I pursue Him.

Father, I'm not afraid of Your bigness—because I know I am welcomed in it all.

Chapter 11

MOVING BEYOND
ME TO US

Worship is a personal thing. But it's also something we do together.

In other words, our responses of worship to God are both personal and corporate. And each kind of response is intertwined with the other.

That's why we say:

Worship is...
our response,
both personal and corporate,
to God—
for who He is!
and what He has done!
expressed in and by the things we say
and the way we live.

Christianity is not an individual sport so much as it is a family affair. Through Christ we've been reconnected to God, and in Him we're linked to each other. We're His body. His people. His family.

Each one of us plays a unique role. We fit with the body in a necessary way.

I'm not talking about joining organized religion, but the organism called the church. If you're a believer in God, He has made you a part of His flock. It's really not your call, but His. He has already made you a member. And a part of your worship is to make a connection with other believers around you.

The primary purpose of the church is worship. At its core, the church exists to glorify God. Without your life and voice, the flock's expression is somehow incomplete.

> The primary purpose of the church is worship.

But even in the corporate setting, worship doesn't begin with a group activity. It begins with our individual responses to what God has revealed to us about Himself. And those responses don't just happen once a week...but day by day.

We aren't designed to operate on a weekly worship cycle, but a moment-by-moment connection of personal worship that's as much a part of our lives as the air we breathe.

PUTTING IT ALL TOGETHER

As we come together with other believers in worship, we can bring that same sense of focus we've had in our daily journey. We bring that same determined devotion.

Most of my life, I thought that you went to church to worship. But now I see that the better approach is to go worshiping to church.

Trust me, church is a lot better when our meetings are filled with people who have been pursuing God for six days before they get there. Church as a "refill" or a "tank-up" is a disaster. Corporate worship works best when we arrive with something to offer God, as opposed to coming only to get something for us.

Church is supposed to be a celebration of our personal journeys with God since we were last together.

Imagine what would happen if each person in the congregation was seeking the face of God throughout the week. Some would encounter sorrow, others major happiness. But all would have a story to tell of God's faithfulness in good times and bad.

What would happen if we came worshiping to church, filled with an awareness of His presence before we reached the door? Well, for one, the lead worshiper's job would be a lot easier! And the intensity of our collective offering would be full on.

Can you see it? All of our personal streams of worship flowing into one surging river. One mighty anthem. A beautiful mosaic, telling an even greater story of who God is and what He's done.

People leave a gathering like that inspired to seek Him as never before. And they come back again bringing worship with them, starting the cycle all over again.

The worship circle is complete. Unbroken.

CONNECTING THE DOTS

We need to overhaul the way we view the Sunday service. Or whenever it is we meet together with others to worship.

Usually we don't give the service a moment's thought until we arrive. We come through the door like we're stopping at the mall. We sit and chat. We wait for someone to guide us before we ever stop and connect with the privilege of it all.

Yet the corporate gathering is a sacred thing. A special thing. A holy thing. Maybe we need bigger buildings after all. Cathedrals that remind us that we're really small and God is really big. Buildings that force us to look up.

Bruce Leafblad, one of the major shapers of my perspective on worship, has a great definition for it. Part of it goes like this: "Worship is centering our mind's attention and our heart's affection on the Lord."

You can't make it any more clear than that.

True worship requires our attention. I know that's difficult in our commercial-driven culture, where our television-trained minds have geared us for a break every seven minutes. But God requires us to love Him with all our minds. His sheer immensity and beauty demand our complete attention.

Have you ever been in a conversation with someone who was constantly looking around while they were talking to you, checking out the scene while you tried to make your point? It makes you just want to walk away, doesn't it?

Why do we think it's any different with God?

When we come to worship together it's imperative that we find God and lock our gaze with His. That's not easy with all the other people in the room. But our primary reason for being there is to see Him. At least it should be.

I don't know about you, but my attention wanders like crazy. For me, the corporate worship experience is a constant round up—chasing down my drifting thoughts and reattaching them to God. So I'm not saying it's easy to stay focused on Him. Just that it's essential.

> It's imperative that we find God and lock our gaze with His.

FACE-TO-FACE, EYE-TO-EYE

As we worship with others, it's important that we find Him, because our attention aims our affection.

We have the amazing potential to shoot arrows of affection into the heart of God. If those arrows are going to hit the target, we have to know where the target is.

And if those arrows from our hearts are going to register with His, they have to be honest and true.

That means we have to think carefully about what we're saying, what we're singing. And who we're singing to. Sometimes we would be better off saying nothing rather than standing there lying to the face of God. Our worship would honor Him more if we just stopped singing and realigned our hearts with His.

I believe that for this to happen we have to connect with God before we arrive. Because worship, in the end, is an intentional thing. Something we set our hearts to do.

So the next time you come to worship with other believers, take a deep breath as you cross the parking lot. Think about the vastness of the God you're coming to meet. Think about His love and grace as you pass through the doors.

And before the worship service begins, begin to worship in your heart.

The key is to come prepared. To come worshiping. To connect with God. To keep our eyes on Him.

WORSHIP IS SO MUCH MORE

You are a worshiper. It's what you do. And you *are* going to worship—no matter what! That's the simple truth of this little book.

Something's going to grab your affection. Someone is going to captivate your attention. One thing is going to rise to the surface of your values and drive your life, aiming your steps and determining your destiny.

But the invitation of God has come to you, inviting you to join those who glorify Him with all of who they are. He's inviting you to discover His infinite worth, giving you the privilege of exalting Him as infinitely worthy.

Through Christ you can breathe again; inhaling the wonder of God that always surrounds you, exhaling words and deeds of praise that reflect all of who He is.

So whether personal or corporate, let's make this what we do. Let's give Him all we are.

The publisher and author would love to hear your comments about this book. *Please contact us at:*
www.lifechangebooks.com

To learn more about the author and the ministry of Passion Conferences, and to see additional resources that will encourage you in being a true worshiper, check out their websites at 268generation.com and 268store.com.

GRATITUDE

Obviously, my worship journey has been shaped and shared by countless others.

Just to mention a few…

Thanks to Sam Perry and Shelley Nirider—and many others who joined our team—early explorers of worship with Shelley and me at Choice Bible Study, Baylor University…the place most of these ideas came to life.

Thanks to Chris Tomlin, Charlie Hall, David Crowder, Matt Redman, and a host of other young lead worshipers, friends, and partners who will shepherd the church for years to come.

Thanks to all at Multnomah Publishers, including Thomas Womack, and the staff of Choice Resources/Passion Conferences, especially my assistant, Jennifer Hill.

QUESTIONS FOR GROUP DISCUSSION

CHAPTER 1: THAT THING WE DO

1. This first chapter defines worship as "our response to what we value most" and "declaring what we value most." Is this a new or larger way of looking at worship for you? In what ways does it make you question or rethink the way you've viewed worship before? Talk openly about this.

2. This chapter also asserts that *all* of us are *always* worshiping. How have you recognized this to be true in your life or the lives of those around you? Can you see it in your choices and actions over the past twenty-four hours?

3. For most people you know, what would you say appear to be the most common objects of their worship, other than God?

4. How can we go about deciding—in an honest and thorough way—what it is we value most in life? How do we effectively and accurately "follow the trail" in order to evaluate how we spend our time? Our affection? Our energy? Our money? Our allegiance?

5. Here are some Scripture passages to explore and discuss together: Colossians 1:15–17; John 1:1–3; 1 Corinthians 8:5–6.

CHAPTER 2: SOMETHING MORE

1. In what memorable ways in your life have you seen that God has been searching for you? How have you noticed His "internal magnet" at work inside you? How have you been aware that He's placed eternity in your heart?

2. Are you fully convinced that God wants you to know who He is and what He's like? Why or why not?

3. In what times of your life have you wrestled most with questions of "ultimate truth"?

4. Talk about the ways in which you identify with the following statement from this chapter: "The journey to God isn't like hopscotch on a chalk-lined sidewalk. It's

more like an awkward groping for someone our eyes cannot see."

5. Think about all that Paul told the Athenians. Which parts of his message to them are most meaningful to you, and why?

6. Some words from God to explore together: Ecclesiastes 3:11; Hebrews 1:1–3; Acts 17:15–34.

Chapter 3: Why Worship Matters

1. *Worship is what God is all about…and God is what worship is all about.* Discuss what those statements mean to you, and your response to them.

2. Knowing that there's a "war" for our worship—that an enemy seeks to steal the love that God longs to receive uniquely from each one of us—how should that affect our thinking about worship and our approach to worship?

3. In what situations can you most easily recognize the battle going on for your values and for your worship?

4. "We become what we worship"—how have you recognized this to be true?

5. We're encouraged in this chapter to "guard" our worship so that we don't squander it "on idols made only with human imagination." What are the best ways to guard our worship?

6. Scripture passages to explore and talk about together: Matthew 4:1–11; Psalm 115:1–8; Revelation 4:8.

Chapter 4: What God Wants Most for You

1. How can God think so highly of Himself and not be egotistical or conceited?
2. "What God wants most for you," this chapter reminds us, "is for you to have a worthy God." What does this tell you most about God? About you?
3. What helps you most to understand and appreciate how the Cross is wonderful? How have you experienced more meaningful worship because of understanding this? How would you describe the place that the Cross should have in our worship?
4. As Jesus talked to the Samaritan woman about worship, He began with the words, "Believe Me…." In our lives, how much does true worship depend on our believing God?
5. Think again about all that Jesus told this woman. Which parts of His message to her are most meaningful to you, and why?
6. Bible passages to explore together: John 4:5–26; Mark 15:33–39; Hebrews 10:22.

Chapter 5: Joining the Ranks of True Worshipers

1. As you've read this book so far, have you found yourself moving toward a greater or more frequent experience of true worship in your life? What have you learned or rediscovered in this book that's already making a difference in your life?

2. This chapter tells us that God is the one who initiates worship, not us. What practical difference do you think this makes?

3. In this chapter we read this statement: "Worship is what spontaneously flows out of us when we come face-to-face with Him." Talk about the most spontaneous experiences of worship that you recall in your own life. How were you "seeing" God in these times? What were you finding to be true about Him?

4. Examine the different phrases in the definition of worship that this chapter gives. Which parts of this definition do you think are probably most important for you to take hold of and remember?

5. Scriptures to explore together: Psalm 95; 150.

CHAPTER 6: FOR WHO HE IS, FOR WHAT HE DOES

1. What are your best answers for the three questions that this chapter begins with: "How can we recover a more exalted view of God in our lives? How can we become the true worshipers we were designed to be? How can we bring back into focus a sense of how awesome God is?"

2. What do you enjoy most about God?

3. When have you been most captivated and excited about God's character—about who He is?

4. When have you been most captivated and excited about God's actions—about what He has done or is doing?

5. What have you found to be the most important factors in protecting and nurturing the intimacy of your relationship with God?

6. Passages from God's Word to explore: Psalm 90:1–2; Romans 11:33–36; Psalm 113; Romans 8:15.

CHAPTER 7: WORSHIP AS A WAY OF LIFE

1. Think about that word *service*. What kind of thoughts and impressions—either positive or negative—does it bring to mind?

2. What motivates you most to want to offer yourself fully to God?

3. This chapter includes this statement: "Grace requires that we bring ourselves, laying our lives before this merciful God." Is grace really grace if it has this or any requirement attached to it? What do you think?

4. How can we know that we're genuinely honoring God and pleasing Him? How can we be sure?

5. Bible passages to explore and experience together: Romans 6:13; 12:1–2.

CHAPTER 8: THROUGH JESUS, ALL THE TIME

1. Why is it so important to keep in our minds and hearts the fact that worship is "through Jesus"? Why does it matter? And what does it mean personally for you to do this?

2. In this book's first chapter, we explored the reality that all of us worship all the time (according to the basic, universal meaning of "worship"). Now as we discover more about the true worship that pleases God, we see Him asking us to worship Him "continually." To offer true worship continually to God, does it help knowing that you're already constantly worshiping anyway?

3. What do you recognize as the most important adjustments needed in your life in order to more continually offer worship to God?

4. Bible passages to explore together: Hebrews 13:15; John 14:6; 15:4–5; Colossians 3:17.

Chapter 9: From Our Lips and from Our Lives

1. What specific forms of "doing good" and "sharing with others" has God given you the opportunity and privilege to live out? How have you sensed God's pleasure in this?

2. What does worshiping God mean—or what *could* it mean—in your own place of work or school?

3. What needs in the lives of people around you seem most urgent to you? What needs in the world around you tend to weigh down your own heart the most?

4. What specific "sacrifices" do you believe God is calling you to make in your life at this time, in order to bring blessing to Him and to people around you?

5. Explore together these Scriptures: Hebrews 13:15–16; 1 Peter 2:5; Philippians 2:12–16.

CHAPTER 10: A PERSONAL PATH TO WORSHIP

1. How difficult is it for you to worship when you're alone with God? What kind of barriers do you typically face? What can help you overcome them?

2. For glimpsing more of God, this chapter suggests a thirty-day personal journey using your Bible, a blank journal, and the basic prayer, "Father, please show me who You are." Have you tried this approach to God? What have you learned?

3. Talk about one or two facets of God's character that have meant the most to you in recent days. How did these come to your attention? How have you grown in your understanding of God?

4. What helps you most to sense that you're drawing close to God?

5. Bible passages to explore together: John 1:18; 2 Corinthians 4:6; Psalm 27:8; 67:1–2.

CHAPTER 11: MOVING BEYOND ME TO US

1. This chapter talks about the need to "go worshiping to church." Is this something you experience in your life? What makes it harder (or easier) for you to come worshiping to church?

2. When do you think it might be appropriate in a corporate worship setting to be silent and not join in with others who are singing and praising God together?

3. How can we keep from being more interested in our experiences of worship than we are in experiencing God Himself?

4. This chapter paints a picture of a congregation that truly seeks God during the week before coming together on Sunday. To what degree is this already happening in your church? What can help cause it to happen more and more?

5. As we conclude the discussion of this book, what do you most want to tell God about the life of worship you desire to live? Talk openly about this before you pray together and actually express those desires to your loving Father in heaven.

6. Explore together these Scriptures: Isaiah 26:8; Psalm 33:1–5; 34:3; 148; Revelation 4:11; 5:12.

QUOTATION SOURCES

CHAPTER 1: THAT THING WE DO
All things made by God and for God—John 1:3; Romans
    11:36; 1 Corinthians 8:6; Colossians 1:16.

CHAPTER 2: SOMETHING MORE
The account of Paul in Athens is found in Acts 17:15–34.
God has placed eternity in our hearts—Ecclesiastes 3:11.
Jesus came to "seek and to save that which was lost"—Luke
    19:10.
Jesus "the radiance of God's glory…"—Hebrews 1:3, NIV.

CHAPTER 3: WHY WORSHIP MATTERS
"Holy, holy, holy is the Lord God…"—Revelation 4:8.
"The heavens are telling of the glory of God.…"—Psalm
    19:1.

"For great is the LORD...."—Psalm 96:4–6, NIV.

Satan falling like lightning—Luke 10:18.

Satan exalting himself more than God—Isaiah 14:13–15.

To exchange "the truth of God for a lie"; "the creature rather than the Creator...."—Romans 1:25.

The account of Jesus being tempted by the enemy in the wilderness is found in Matthew 4:1–11.

"Not to us, O LORD, not to us...."; "But their idols are silver and gold...."; "Those who make them will be like them...."—Psalm 115:1–8, NIV.

Changed into God's very likeness (glory) from encounter to encounter—2 Corinthians 3:18.

CHAPTER 4: WHAT GOD WANTS MOST FOR YOU

That we might "declare the praise of Him who called you out of darkness..."—1 Peter 2:9, NIV.

The account of the conversation beside the well between Jesus and the Samaritan woman is found in John 4:1–26, NIV.

David said: "I waited patiently for the LORD..."—Psalm 40:1–3, NIV.

"The Wonderful Cross"—this phrase is used in a Chris Tomlin adaptation of the classic worship song "When I Survey the Wondrous Cross" (Isaac Watts, 1707;

adaptation by Chris Tomlin in *The Noise We Make,*
Six Steps Records/Sparrow Records, 2001).

Jesus *becoming* sin and shame—2 Corinthians 5:21.

The centurion saying, "Truly this man was the Son of
God"—Mark 15:39.

CHAPTER 5: JOINING THE RANKS OF TRUE WORSHIPERS

"True worshipers"—John 4:23.

"Great is the LORD and greatly to be praised"—Psalms
18:3; 29:2; 45:1; 48:1; 96:4; 104:1.

CHAPTER 6: FOR WHO HE IS, FOR WHAT HE DOES

"Before the mountains were born…"—Psalm 90:2.

"Oh, the depth of the riches…"—Romans 11:33.

"Who has known the mind of the Lord?…"—Romans
11:34–36, NIV.

"Lift your eyes and look to the heavens…"—Isaiah 40:26,
NIV.

"In the beginning God created…"—Genesis 1:1.

"For since the creation of the world God's invisible
qualities…"—Romans 1:20, NIV.

"Holy, holy, holy is the Lord Almighty"—Revelation 4:8;
Isaiah 6:3.

"Who is like the LORD our God…"—Psalm 113:5

As David said, "intimately acquainted"—Psalm 139:3.

"The heavens are telling of the glory of God"—Psalm 19:1.

The rocks God has made are capable of singing songs —Luke 19:40.

His Spirit cries within our hearts, "Abba! Father!"—Romans 8:15; Galatians 4:6. In Aramaic (the common language used in Jesus' day), *Abba* is an endearing term of closeness and intimacy that a child would use for his dad.

CHAPTER 7: WORSHIP AS A WAY OF LIFE

Paul "beseeching" us "in view of God's mercy…" —Romans 12:1, NIV.

"These people honor me with their lips…"—Matthew 15:8, NIV.

God has given us "life and breath and all things"—Acts 17:25.

The "reasonable" thing to do—Romans 12:1, KJV.

Contemporary paraphrase, Romans 12:1—*The Message.*

"It's not the words I sing, but me I bring"—Louie Giglio, 2001.

CHAPTER 8: THROUGH JESUS, ALL THE TIME

"Through Him then, let us continually offer…"—
   Hebrews 13:15.
Christ offered "one sacrifice for sins for all time"—
   Hebrews 10:12.

CHAPTER 9: FROM OUR LIPS AND FROM OUR LIVES

"Through [Jesus] then, let us continually offer…"
   —Hebrews 13:15–16.
What comes out of the mouth is actually coming from
   the heart—Matthew 15:18.
David says, "I will bless the LORD at all times…"—Psalm
   34:1.
"Shout to the north and the south…"—words and music
   by Martin Smith (Curious? Music/EMI Christian
   Music Publishing, 1995).

CHAPTER 10: A PERSONAL PATH TO WORSHIP

"All the treasures of wisdom and knowledge"—Colossians
   2:3.

CHAPTER 11: MOVING BEYOND ME TO US

Bruce Leafblad's definition in full (as given in his course
"Introduction to Church Music" at Southwestern
Baptist Theological Seminary, 1983): "Worship is
communion with God in which believers, by grace,
center their mind's attention and their heart's
affection on the Lord, humbly glorifying God in
response to His greatness and His Word."
He alone is worthy—Revelation 4:11; 5:12.

It's hard to spot when you're laughing